The Boundary Stone

The Boundary Stone
C von Hassett

Copyright © 2022 by C von Hassett
Text © 2012 C von Hassett

Paperback ISBN-13: 978-1-956503-80-7
eBook ISBN-13: 978-1-956503-81-4

All characters appearing in this work are fictitious. Any resemblance to real persons, living or dead, is purely coincidental.
No part of this book may be reproduced in any form or by any electronic or mechanical means, including information storage and retrieval systems, without written permission from the publisher or the author, except in the case of a reviewer, who may quote brief passages embodied in critical articles or in a review.

Waterside Productions
2055 Oxford Ave
Cardiff, CA 92007
www.waterside.com

To Rachel

Nothing of you but breakage,
scattered bone, a length of which
I lift.

Black, charred, one with all else,

its drippings run with light,
its marrows the fats of luminous night...

I

Around the city, the tunnels. These,
ancient waters turned thoroughfare turned cataclysmic
blaze that took houses and the child and the earth lay
blackened and thousands had rooted to the soil,
fuliginous and trunked.

The trails through arroyos and those in the hills become
deadpaths of bone and darked plainswood, skeletal saguaros
and sparceoak,

and the peaks above and the towering basalts, where tree
stone and sun and calendar steps, scripted piers, altars of let,
stairglyphs told to temple mouths,

                all in the ashfall stood spectral.

And I took to the lapsed earth, to the soil
of dark crystal, and I wandered through ashfall
and was mirrored in coaltimber and laid foot
to a smoky plane and there found an out.

A cenote dropped through desert glass, tremendous
at its edge.

Where once its waters, now an absolute fall
and darkness fell also in its depths.

                     And I leaned
and stepped forth and settled to the unlighted air
and tumbled,

your flame to my chest,

and there was nothing but fall until the visions,
of you and of those more fierce.

And then the lights.

And they nimbused and hung and took to the walls
and leapt filiform and synapsed bulbar and borne
were long flashes that held but shortly and none
shone brighter than yours and to yours I held
certain and I alighted and laid to the nether stone
and slept.

I lay still and many times passed and time unspooled and was no more.

And I stood with your flame and went out upon the open stone.

II

These depths. A great plane of waters
and the waters had gone and stone lay in sheets
and some stood erect and this body of rock
was shoaled in veins gone wide and come again
and they plaited and went off and all led
to still deeper darkness.

And with yours as needle, as fire and warmth,
I went in to the veins and went down.

The course of riverbeds and rapids laid of rock, settled streams of sand,

and all were silent and had been.

These waters from another world wandered
and fell and disappeared into another.

And I in them followed and fell, past the lope
of sediment past lime and the stone of silt.
Between plates massive and shelving and stacked
slant.

And long and lilting shadows were thrown yet
none stood the rock nor bore they witness to
being and these shadows in the silence fell away
without trace.

They fell to a great sunderance in the earth where one
element long yet passed for another and left was
a vast ocean of sand and rock and space without end
and on above the skies sprent astral, as if the dark and
nether firmament had by seers been spiracled to
reference, if just, their own luminous suns to the circuit
of all others.

And there began the glyphs.

These the prefigurements of what had yet come and of what since'd passed in lack and in plenty and in the extinction of all and again it was scribed and again all had gone and the walls went on.

They fanned longward in arc and they rose very high and so the glyphs. On these stood a desiccated land of fire and rock and there were waters else and the skies pitched, crazed with the couplings of every darkness, and they slavered and spilled and threw splints of light and the land fell abysmal beneath a glistening sheet.

The waters did fall. They fell to the main and fell
deeper still and they arose of lesser than from whence
befallen and therewith the land stood the seas
and puzzled apiece.

And no reach of shore took nearer to the next nor
any fixed destiny in the mere world.

And the waters soon panned and tiered the lands and one
man, skinned in mammal, walked thwart and sat new
shores and all to his eye were fertile and green.

And this man sat and fell tilt his skull and longly he halved
and from his loins bore what? its fleshy bulb astave,
its black and hollow globes cocked askew, peering not
to its nor any world other.

And this,
      child,
        this son,
had its ear to the soil and no mouth to be spoken of for it
was utterly disjoined and aft to its skull and was manned
and articulated by some verdant palm come as sapling from
the soil.

From the skies to the seas plunged a mammoth beast
and it took to the land and ranged it wide,
its vast plains, its belting greens.

It came upon the man lying back, the child faceless
and bent, his skull gripped, fists knuckled to the soil,

and laid its hoof to the downfather's heart and fell him
through and it mounted the boy and drove him into
the standing wild and doubled him there.

The boy many year reared sentry his mount and was
fostered its upon and upon it grew. He grew to set
foot and finger to the soil and there lifted flint and with

its shave reached back and severed from the beast its
phallus and took the life and ate and too was with child.

And this boy come man sat cold and bade fire and bore
another, a girl.

And they as one raised staff and shelter and around
them came other slippings who sat blue to the flames,
cold they in that primal camp.

Soon a common stood the fire and it burned.

And they as coal stood fixed and beyond them yond baned
grass and darks and shadows lurked and not one still soul
turned from the light but for their black and misset eyes.

And a blazing hand fell from the sky and touched the man whose eyes lit.

And he turned to the grass and entered its darkness and was gone.

In those darks he slew and was slain and he fell to the deeps and traveled and fell still and killed as before one of some other temper.

There in the darkness he was utterly transformed and he arose as other, with fire and touch and without word,

and he was raised and divined and did not pass again.

The wall went on, and on did the tale. And the rock seemed wholly without end until it rent sharp and wrested from the whole and between its lengths a massive stone had rounded off entire and it did not sit the sand but hung afloat, perfect and still.

On it as prints, evanescing and luminous, the doubleglyphs of what had just passed and of what was beyond and they blinked and were gone and blinked again above, these same.

And directly the front and always on the round sat a prince golden beneath a tree. This tree had rooted the soil and had rooted above and it took to his spine and he did not move as did all else.

And he sat lone. Above his bluely bald head a myriad worlds were born and turned and wove as one and fell again away.

These worlds and this man were not different on the globe nor in the depiction one but were of dream and dreamer in dream and all but the dreamer slept and dreamt.

And he, palm raised, passed hand through many worlds and many times and laid finger to the heart of another who slept not again and did not dream for he was not then born and not of death.

And this had been even in birth and in his ever passings.

And he with the prince went to light so pure that it was pure on that rock and I knew then that I was of matter other, of darkness so black, so singular, that your flame went dim upon my know and I could not print the rock with my image for my soul

The story ran the stone without orient or onset and on it in a single point of light was a congress of mind and ceaseless being and all knew light for all were. And still.

And this of beginning was nothing and was nothing else.

Yet disrupt parted all in one breech of fire that slumbered still the light and all were left blind and all at once lost and seen thereon were shadows and shapes and reached for to that veil of black and touched and felt was flesh and earth and its unfailing lack and in such felt lack such the fall and, too, its counter came to pass. And so with, time.

And one by one the one of light wakes
dreamt ones slept in this.

The channel took me on, to the sure and running darks.
Along faulted rock. And the glyphs picked up and soils
there rendered squared and fields were drawn, stock
and shed, the spooling of fiber, the black of wood,

and not cloth nor plenty ended the kill of old,
for in man was slaughter and all that went wild wove
to yore and the hunt did not cease and the soil won
from beast was bored and metals unearthed and altered.

And one man on turned ground knelt, his head craned
hind, and from his mouth dehisced such fire
and the spread of light and the skies loured and from on
high the sun went whole and darkness fell apace.

And this of one.

And on those walls was a history yet to pass yet its story
no end other than of what had passed before and has since
come upon the scorched city above.

Others were follow. A sweeping arcana through which the fictions of time and the dream of man parading each and vanishing each and each to the next as if no other would come nor other come before had in their faint permanence come codified.

And these last seemed laid by some great and heavy hand that set to reveal all yet swept all obscure in its pass, leaving but phantom delineations to be perused
and apprehended with no method to forestall nor forecast alter.

And then their end.

The channel went on.

It stepped and rove and branched round stones
and ran the leants and stacks of shelves and on
to slopes and to the slanted earth, to blacksands
and clays, to the distant cliffs beyond.

It fell with your flame to the cants of others
and there ran deeper as ghost.

III

You flowered off, your light.
Farther the bearing sparks.

Winds. They've taken you to smoke.

Your bone, now embering, gone glassy
and sharp,

through my heart pressed for fear its loss.

And darkness is stark, pitched
by winds and terrible warps and breakage.

The air metaled. It snaps and cracks
and whips in chains and ice is in chains, lashing.

And its crystals lay skin to the weigh of flense,
its felted warmths, and the way were your follow
is off and balance off in the slurry blackness.

And ice hung in spines and from the walls on edge

sheers touch and but wholly unhands. Nor is there
foot to what lies.

And it needles dull and culls what blood what sense
what list and sharp.

Nothing seems pass, neither the winds.

Yet end beyond mere moment's cast comes
windbreak and rest.

Here, my love, darkness sleeps the inner stones
spread cool like orbs paled in naught,

and it pools lightless and lulls and lopes things
seen to the falsened eye.

Darkness comes abreath, dips were it pressed,

blacks to gas and floats and lies flat. It flaps
from points fixed and falls again.

And winds on it lift and tongues offwhere lilt,
of earth or of dream, your voice in allure.

And they are stopping and altogether lovely.

Falsewings strike above. Rumors of wind.

From the seamless ceils, a sweep unseals, combing highs.

Their quicken.

And shafts there deepen, furnace redly from black, when with come winds and absence darkness, sheds of light.

And in a luminous gust,
your figure,

supple and lovely, lifting, leading up,
through rock.

Their come,
rains of shadow and umbered sheets of wind.

Things stir. Bottomlight, the icy floor.

Sparks stand the air, gesture, are swallowed
with the dyings into an otherless dark.

But shortly. A great sucking bears down through the earth and the ice reblooms and the air bloodies. Light anew mats the walls, squares and grids and arches longly through space. It angles out, lays flat to the air, doubles and does again and onward high in platforms of light, perfect each in interval and geometry, and they rotate as one and rise still.

At once the whole folds and to elements same
it spheres, orbits elliptic. It spins, burns to some
other brightness and bursts.

And it sembles to flame and fast spreads, running
rock and skipping ice and pouring the walls molten
until it pools.

In the cavern central a bonefire sets and sat its round
are seven not of stone not of light but fleshed
and elder and nor they flesh nor stone but light
of every cast and they are but mere rock in this aught
deviation, everbeings vapors to the fire.

And their eyes to mine burn and against the blaze
burn black. And a decrepit stands, the walls bow
and strand. They slip, weave mandalic. And charts
there glister and the way with one hand lift is lit.

And this wizened and wavering being presses his palms
and from his heart pours pure a watering light and it
is I and the immensity of love and this light I know
and have known and, as just, he with the others are gone
and the crepitate fire crumples and lowlight spreads.

And winds drag off and iris tarries and silence again
measures.

And I listen for your breath, break
crystal on ice, make my way through
the veilbreaks up.

IV

Through switches of darkness and rock charged electric, loom drippings and belting auroras. Their curtains lay in luminous folds that windwhipped fall and sweep gentle the slopes.

They pale cliffwall and wall and inward roll and swirl long and wrap loosely in coils and rise again against the elevate and up as streamers or maelstrom spectra stood round poles greenly magnetic and going blue to whirling ribbons of red.

And the river below rises whitegassed and plasmic and shapes itself in spectral forms.

Strewn the way are brethren shatters and those yet
foresting above. Their glazings lain amid limbs
and trunks. Some in mirror to their own.

Alone, a great fallen dripping stands true in the sand.
Others oblique to the fallen world.

To on high, the wooded gulch, to plateland stepped indigo and spread steely blue and barrened by winds stanched from upland throats.

And tables from the earth pull through floats of silver and banding whites and hang magnetic against a dark and drawing firmament.

And electric winds lay static the sand and strands of iron stand and flit and sway on fragile stems and they cluster as one and lift and parasol and twirl in the air and come intimate and in and lift again on toes balletic.

And all is pageant above the sands, which from bay reblacken and give again, and these their givings their presence to the winds are taken to the slopes and still deeper taken.

And I their way move opposite, through highland blacks and terrible winds and rock hammered from its origins absolute to stand as such in darkness same.

The valley below lies in changeless shadow,
this from peaks running vast and chined and
abacked by what neverrising sun seemed in
misorbit beyond.

Onward the land lavenders and strias threadlike
and stones rise there-lumined, scrolled in such
tongues singular and impenetrable and heeled
upon by charts and grotesqué that speak of
sconcegrottos where-else.

Canyons and pavilions. The valley defiles.

There but to margins of stone and straight rising rock, a strip of sand in the deepening lengths.

Sand.

Deeper still the slumberwater, its slow pitchings
and dream risings, its crumpled posts and drop-offs.

And the dozing canyon rolls and turns and yawns
through beds of talus and molts itself to sandglass
and falls and falls to worlds very changed –

floats of sulfur and chokedamp, lampgas and ash
and steam vents hissing wild. Dimly hung globes,
some ochery luminous. These brighten in move
and dim again near dunes, at dark stands of rock,
geyserite stood in glimmering mounds.

And flows of magma, mute beneath the din, blister
thin and seethe, flare upon its pilings and bank longly
toward an outland rim, then drop silently away.

And pools of differing quake in reds and muddy
yellows, greens that lobe and faintly cough.

Beyond, a great molten sea.

Upon its berth stretch stonevault looms, wracked
and doomed like argosy slains lost in firth,
their whited archings in smoke and crumble, their
hulls wholly cracked.

And this sea with its carry is fell upon by such
drippings fibrous and massive that finger down
from the deeps above, some in neap column,
others as gallow for numen specter
pendent if not in penance above the firelasts.

It is held this sea by charred headland and cliffs
rising high, shoulders to a severed land spread
farly and white, of chalkflats and pulver and but
a single rock sat marbling and large and perfectly
round and to its setting quite stark.

The earth around lies otherwise shapeless, unbroken,
entirely without end

                              Till lo!

what breath stitched to remembrance takes hold
with light held in streaks ascending green through
collapsing space.

          Above a wink, a rain of powders,
and darkness stops down

and all are borne the waters of dream

V

To reawaken, deeper.
The world fallen wholly to another.

Lightfall, like prayer.
Beneath which I lie.

Till you, my heart, lift me and lead.

        Still down.

Through lairs and lower, your needle as stead. Through sponge groves and waters in skein. To an opening draped in blooms.

Within, a cavern altogether turned.

Its dome rathers down and is darkly pooled and on it, light, were it elsewhere lunar. It pales, this light, belts cobalt and cools. And pupiless crescents lie the pools, glassen amongst the changelings and blue reflected to deeply black.

And below is abloom and in magnificent erupt, with nightshades the walls and purplebell in fall, with veronicas and jacob's ladder and giant pitcher plants lit. With reeds to the necks of nun's-hood swung in robes beneath the nimbus light.

To these, a sort of swallowtail, that lilt and link and lay at watering lips, lift as if from glass and spread in floral sprays. They tuck to the lianas, to the glories of moonflower, morning, golden gingerlilies and day.

They swirl above butterfly and snakemouth and vines bearing vanilla, around orchids of another in lightsome spills.

Their tressings tip in reds and savage yellows and oranges burnt to going black and lamped by such pollinial stocks stood vivid and whorled like tendering panicles to an apian convoke.

Their spreadings dip and weave and rove along the floor and hook to the spines of eels haloing the wets and upon those same risen from holes to slip the waters mindful, electric, coolly cyanic, in move of sponge or slug or a star in colored plays or snails neon charged or seacups inking.

And they choke these down and jerk their heads and tongue the running
waters and move on, between rock and charged metals, where to these they flash, dim and go dark.

One roils ablaze, its tail deep in throat. Others to still deeper holes, where I with they toward some trebling draw.

Cascades of scarlet come the stonechutes to these
quenched seas. And waters from above stand loud
and sheet the leaning adamant and vanish
to the clovens to the very oblivions of the earth.

And livid stonefish and the eels now diminished
lie still. And all the forgot, their pulpy lids
and bloodless eyes gape the waters and walls
and flux blind beneath the falls and strobe to
the general splash and their cool and constant
emissions pearl the incarcerate waters.

And organ-lanterned fish slake the stones by
thousands and float in cistern pools in what call
of atavism or hearkening to the voids since been
cast. And for these and the others there is but wait
and watch and utter remain, as if planted they to
the very rock and rooted their souls to the nether
stays and the waters abide.

And lightless their amongst, one I near, its eye
lapsed and in lee, its blackness glint,

and it pulls and pulls therein and pulls me in,
past its lens and lightpoints billioned, and into
lightways other it sends.

VI

In these the warmths of recast come, emanates
of darkness and sourceless black light. The vast
unfold of space.

Upon it, luminosities in limpid pools and fountains
in arcing blacks.

And my eyes receive their plenish and pours and
light I breathe and in sense become.

And thunder crashes through radiance and crystal'd
vision and clarity pured. And blazing forth

                                        your face,

blueblack and bone-adorned, your wrathful gaze,
your clucking tongue.

And a droplet your midbrow wells and falls
and mirrors emptiness and light in emptiness
and no figure nor your own makes its round

yet through perfect stillness it falls and perfectly
still through stretchless space.

Within it, worldings new – of move and extent,
shifting displays, a groundless way.

And to my heart it comes and intakes and to yours
long darkened touches light once more.

Lobing silver, you total to light, absorbing all.

Within I blink, move faint from breath through a magnificence of space, through brilliant blackness and great quaking plates, through forming pressures, phenomenal shifts, ruptures felt,

against walls of darkness so incredibly dense and through, to dimensions angular and somehow sharp. Through terrains unseen and steep and sharply up, a steppe without footing or floor but for the enormity of space beneath, its splits and fiery strikes that crack and cascade and tendril through regions far off.

On. A ground transparent and floating and swarmed upon by singeing elementals and storming droplets downed blue from bodies strung black and massive above, a ground undered clear through with infinite worlds and satellites and scores of ruddy suns suspended blackbound and mute through spheres liquesce and darkly luminous,

and you palm the ill-illumed, shape yourself flat
along papers of space and in darknesses absolute
you move mercurial through densities terrible
in their ferocity and of stifling malevolence

yours through regenerate darks and many worlds,
where in these and each but instants pass and each,
still, eternal space and the essence of light and
glorious beings, their retinues supremely luminous

through these with you to realms of blackness so
revealed that balance regained is to their brights belied.

VII

Peril the light your crystal lure. Perish return the allure of black. And disorient is fast, the new darks.

And my heart in their geographies falls weigh and want of rest. Vagues their replica. It founders new.
Of doubt. Fear. Darkings of its nature newly in spring.

And their tones and tonics well and saturate and leave stain my palms and metallic the tongue, specter voicings, misshape the visables till they're formless and rotary.

And all falls otherwise dark and offwards you stand and I can no more.

                                                And I yield.

Your streak goes high on the azimuth.

And the way has not been nor been beyond.

Your splendor at the spread of dawn is streamed
and unobstruct and lays out warm. And changes of
darkness fall clear and darkness clears.

And sears of skin shed to fiery rares and waver like
nimbus orbs beatified and in behold, and my eyes
to these scale and open and through whence my crown
a fiery beam and from my heart, light.

And light is become.

My heart,
its organ and emanation, its clearlight pours.

And I in its beams bear lovely aloft and one
with the opens and with all, one, in wondrous
unveil and newly with yours, one.

                And light is to light

                            ours,
                songing the everlast.

The Boundary Stone

Other books by C von Hassett
Entering the Mind

www.ingramcontent.com/pod-product-compliance
Lightning Source LLC
Chambersburg PA
CBHW070655050426
42451CB00008B/361